modern readers · stage 1

Nicholas's Prize

Eduardo Amos
Elisabeth Prescher
Ernesto Pasqualin

3rd edition

Richmond

© EDUARDO AMOS, ELISABETH PRESCHER, ERNESTO PASQUALIN, 2004

Richmond

Coordenação editorial: *Véra Regina A. Maselli, Kylie Mackin*
Assistência editorial: *Gabriela Peixoto Vilanova*
Coordenação de produção gráfica: *Fernando Dalto Degan*
Coordenação de revisão: *Estevam Vieira Lédo Jr.*
Revisão: *Denise Ceron*
Edição de arte: *Christiane Borin*
Projeto gráfico de miolo e capa: *Ricardo Van Steen Comunicações e Propaganda Ltda./Oliver Fuchs*
Ilustrações de miolo e capa: *Murilo*
Diagramação: *EXATA Editoração*
Coordenação de bureau: *Américo Jesus Arriate Teixeira*
Tratamento de imagens: *Ideraldo Araújo de Melo*
Saída de filmes: *Hélio P. de Souza Filho, Marcio H. Kamoto*
Coordenação de produção industrial: *Wilson Aparecido Troque*
Impressão e acabamento:*Forma Certa Gráfica Digital*
Lote: 783424
Cód.: 12037231

Dados Internacionais de Catalogação na Publicação (CIP)
(Câmara Brasileira do Livro, SP, Brasil)

Amos, Eduardo
  Nicholas's prize / Eduardo Amos, Elisabeth Prescher, Ernesto Pasqualin ; (ilustrações Murilo). — 3. ed. — São Paulo : Moderna, 2003. — (Modern readers ; stage 1)

  1. Inglês (Ensino fundamental) I. Prescher, Elisabeth. II. Pasqualin, Ernesto. III. Murilo. IV. Título. V. Série.

03-3362   CDD-372.652

Índices para catálogo sistemático:
1. Inglês : Ensino fundamental   372.652

ISBN 85-16-03723-1

Reprodução proibida. Art.184 do Código Penal e Lei 9.610 de 19 de fevereiro de 1998.

Todos os direitos reservados.

RICHMOND
SANTILLANA EDUCAÇÃO LTDA.
Rua Padre Adelino, 758, 3º andar — Belenzinho
São Paulo — SP — Brasil — CEP 03303-904
www.richmond.com.br
2023

Impresso no Brasil

Chapter 1

Bob Nelson — Good evening, ladies and gentlemen! Welcome to The Bob Nelson Show. I am Bob Nelson and this is our Million-Dollar Game. Tonight is a special night. There is a super prize for three correct answers. Yes, ladies and gentlemen, only three correct answers. And here is tonight's contestant. Please welcome Nicholas Benson.

Bob Nelson — Hi, Nicholas! Welcome to our show.
Nicholas — Thank you, Bob.
Bob Nelson — Where are you from, Nicholas?
Nicholas — I'm from Buffalo, New York.
Bob Nelson — Here are three envelopes. In each envelope there are three questions. With three correct answers, the prize is yours. The prize is yours, Nicholas!
Nicholas — What is it?
Bob Nelson — It's a surprise, but it's a great prize. It's a wonderful prize, Nicholas! Now, which envelope? Number one, number two, or number three?
Nicholas — Mmm... number two.
Bob Nelson — Number two, ladies and gentlemen. OK, here is envelope number two. And now the first question. Are you ready, Nicholas?
Nicholas — Yes, I am.
Bob Nelson — Question number one: "What is Burkina Faso?" A. The name of a flower. B. The name of a country. C. The name of a rock singer.

Nicholas — It's the name of a ... mmm...
Bob Nelson — Twenty seconds!
Nicholas — The answer is B, the name of a country.
Bob Nelson — Your answer is correct! Very good, Nicholas. Burkina Faso is the name of a country in Africa. Now, question number two: "What is the capital of China?" A. Hong-Kong. B. Singapore. C. Beijing.

Nicholas — It is... hmm...

Bob Nelson — What is the capital of China, Nicholas? The name of the city. Hong-Kong, Singapore, or Beijing?

Nicholas — Beijing is the capital of China.

Bob Nelson — Are you sure?

Nicholas — Yes, I'm sure. The answer is C, Beijing. The capital of China is Beijing.

Bob Nelson — Your answer is correct! Beijing is the capital of China. Hong-Kong is in China, but it isn't the capital. And Singapore is not in China. Congratulations, Nicholas! You're right.

Now, our last question. One more correct answer and the super prize is yours. Be careful! This is a hard question. Are you ready for the last question, Nicholas?

Nicholas — Yes, I'm ready.

Bob Nelson — OK, this is your last question: "How many countries have borders with Brazil?" A. Five. B. Ten. C. Eight.

Nicholas — That's hard.

Bob Nelson — Yes, it's very hard.

Nicholas — Mmm...

Bob Nelson — Fifteen seconds.

Nicholas — Well...

Bob Nelson — Ten seconds.

Nicholas — B is the answer.

Bob Nelson — B?

Nicholas — Yes, the answer is B. Ten countries have borders with Brazil.

Bob Nelson — Right! Right! Right! That's great, Nicholas! Congratulations! And now the mystery prize. Are you ready?

Nicholas — Yes. What is it?

Bob Nelson — Guess.

Nicholas — A bicycle?

Bob Nelson — No.

Nicholas — A motorcycle?

Bob Nelson — No. Your prize is... a trip.

Nicholas — A trip? Where to? Miami?

Bob Nelson — No, to a different place.

Nicholas — Paris?

Bob Nelson — No, an exotic place.

Nicholas — Rio?

Bob Nelson — No. Your prize is a trip to Saint Lucia. It is seven days with a family in Saint Lucia.

Nicholas — Saint Lucia? Where is that?

Bob Nelson — Saint Lucia is a small island in the Caribbean.

Nicholas — The Caribbean? Wow!

Bob Nelson — Well, that is it, ladies and gentlemen. Thank you very much. See you next week on The Bob Nelson Show.

FACT FILE — SAINT LUCIA

Saint Lucia is an island in the Caribbean 26 miles north of Saint Vincent and only 21 miles south of Martinique. It is a small island with only 616 square kilometers.

There are about 160,145 inhabitants. Ninety percent of the population is of African descent.

The capital of Saint Lucia is Castries. Saint Lucians are considered British citizens because their country is part of the British Commonwealth.

English is the official language, but at home and on the streets, the people speak a language called patois.

Saint Lucia is famous for its beautiful beaches.

Chapter 2

Nicholas is at the airport in Saint Lucia now. The Williams family is there too.

Mr Williams — Hello, Nicholas! Welcome to Saint Lucia. I am Guy Williams and this is my wife Alison.
Nicholas — Hello, nice to meet you.
Mrs Williams — Welcome to our family.
Nicholas — Thanks, Mrs Williams.
Mrs Williams — Oh, this is our daughter Rachel.
Nicholas — Hi, Rachel!
Rachel — Hi, Nicholas! This is my brother Emory.
Nicholas — Hello, Emory! Mmm... Are you two twins?
Emory and Rachel — Yes, we are.

Nicholas is at the Williams' house now. It is in the middle of a small banana plantation.

Emory — This is our farm, Nick. It's a banana plantation.

Nicholas — It's beautiful. Is it big?

Emory — Not really.

Rachel — Nothing is really big in Saint Lucia.

Emory — What about your house? Is it on a farm, too?

Nicholas — No, it's in the city. I live in an apartment in Buffalo, New York.

Rachel — How's your school?

Nicholas — My school is OK. I like it. My mother is a cook in the school cafeteria.

Emory — Neat! There is no cafeteria at our school. We are in school from seven in the morning till noon. What are your school hours in Buffalo?

    Nicholas — From eight in the morning till three in the afternoon. Is your school in the city?

    Emory — No, it's a rural school. We have regular subjects like English and Math and technical subjects too.

    Nicholas — What are the technical subjects?

    Rachel — Well, we have Planting Techniques, Soil Conservation and First Aid.

    Nicholas — And what are your favorite subjects?

    Rachel — English and Math.

    Nicholas — I like Geography very much and I like Art too. What about you, Emory?

    Emory — My favorite subject is break time.

Chapter 3

After a week in Saint Lucia, Nicholas is back home. He is the special guest on The Bob Nelson Show. The questions tonight are about Saint Lucia, but it's not a game.

Bob Nelson — Ladies and gentlemen, please welcome Nicholas Benson again. He is back from his trip to Saint Lucia. Well, Nicholas, are you ready for some questions about Saint Lucia?

Nicholas — Yes, Mr Nelson.

Bob Nelson — So, tell us about Saint Lucia.

Nicholas — It's beautiful and the people are really nice.

Bob Nelson — Really! Who is the president of Saint Lucia?

Nicholas — There is no president in Saint Lucia, only a governor and a prime minister.

Bob Nelson — No president? How come?

Nicholas — Saint Lucia is a member of the British Commonwealth. The Head of State is Queen Elizabeth II, of England.

Bob Nelson — Very interesting. Now, one last question: "What is the main economic activity in Saint Lucia?"

Nicholas — Agriculture. Bananas are the main export product of the island. But tourism is also a very important economic activity.

Bob Nelson — Well, thank you very much, Nicholas. Congratulations, Buffalo! Your boy is really smart. Now, ladies and gentlemen, it's time for tonight's contestant. Please, welcome ...

KEY WORDS

The meaning of each word corresponds to its use in the context of the story (see page number 00)

about (8) aproximadamente
back (12) de volta
border (6) fronteira
break time (11) intervalo
British Commonwealth (8) Comunidade Britânica
cafeteria (10) cantina
call, called (8) chamar
contestant (3) concorrente
citizen (8) cidadão
cook (10) cozinheira
country (4) país
daughter (9) filha
farm (10) fazenda
first aid (11) primeiros socorros
game (3) jogo
guess (7) adivinhar
guest (12) convidado
hard (6) difícil
Head of State (12) Chefe de Estado
island (7) ilha
last (6) última
main (13) principal
nice (12) simpático
noon (10) meio-dia
only (3) apenas
place (7) lugar
planting (11) plantio
prime minister (12) primeiro-ministro

prize (3) prêmio
ready (4) pronto
right (6) correto
second (5) segundo
singer (4) cantor
smart (13) esperto
soil (11) solo
south (8) sul
square (8) quadrado
subject (11) matéria escolar
till (11) até
too (9) também
trip (7) viagem
twin (9) gêmeo
week (7) semana
which (4) qual
wife (9) esposa
with (4) com
wonderful (4) maravilhoso

Expressions

Are you sure? (6) Tem certeza?
Be careful! (6) Cuidado!
Congratulations! (6) Parabéns!
How come? (12) Como assim?
I'm ready... (6) Estou pronto...
Ladies and gentlemen... (3) Senhoras e senhores
Neat! (10) Muito legal!
Nice to meet you (9) Prazer em conhecê-lo.

ACTIVITIES

Before reading

1. Read the title of the book and the back cover.
   Nicholas's prize is:
   ( ) a T.V.   ( ) a trip

While Reading

Chapter One

2. Read page 3 and complete the table below.

Program	The Bob Nelson Show
Presenter	
Contestant	

3. Read pages 4 to 6. Tick the correct answers.
   a) What is Burkina Faso?
      ( ) The name of a flower.
      ( ) The name of a country.
      ( ) The name of a rock singer.
   b) What is the capital of China?
      ( ) Hong Kong ( ) Singapore   ( ) Beijing
   c) How many countries have borders with Brazil?
      ( ) Five   ( ) Ten   ( ) Eight

4. Read page 8 and complete the FACT FILE about Saint Lucia.

   Fact File – Saint Lucia

Population	
Capital	
Official Language	
Size	

Chapter Two

5. Read pages 10 and 11. Complete the information about Nicholas, Emory and Rachel.

Emory and Rachel	Nicholas
1. They are in school from 7.00 till	He is in school from 8.00 till ....
2. Rachel's favorite subjects are .... and .... Emory's favorite subject is	His favorite subjects are .... and ....

Chapter Three

6. Read pages 12 and 13 and complete the facts about Saint Lucia. Then talk to a friend and complete the information about Brazil.

Fact File — Saint Lucia

Fact File — Brazil

Head of State —	**Head of State —**
President — There is no president, but there is a prime minister	**President —**
Important Economic Activity —	**Important Economic Activities —**

After Reading (Optional Activities)

7. Compare your school schedule with the school schedules of Emory, Rachel and Nicholas. What is the same? What is different?

8. In which countries is English the official language? In which countries is Portuguese the official language?

16